A NOTE TO PARENTS

When your children are ready to "step into reading," giving them the right books is as crucial as giving them the right food to eat. **Step into Reading Books** present exciting stories and information reinforced with lively, colorful illustrations that make learning to read fun, satisfying, and worthwhile. They are priced so that acquiring an entire library of them is affordable. And they are beginning readers with a difference—they're written on five levels.

Early Step into Reading Books are designed for brand-new readers, with large type and only one or two lines of very simple text per page. **Step 1 Books** feature the same easy-to-read type as the Early Step into Reading Books, but with more words per page. **Step 2 Books** are both longer and slightly more difficult, while **Step 3 Books** introduce readers to paragraphs and fully developed plot lines. **Step 4 Books** offer exciting nonfiction for the increasingly independent reader.

The grade levels assigned to the five steps—preschool through kindergarten for the Early Books, preschool through grade 1 for Step 1, grades 1 through 3 for Step 2, grades 2 through 3 for Step 3, and grades 2 through 4 for Step 4—are intended only as guides. Some children move through all five steps very rapidly; others climb the steps over a period of several years. Either way, these books will help your child "step into reading" in style!

*To Dr. Francine G. Patterson
and the staff of the Gorilla Foundation and to the
staff of NYZS/The Wildlife Conservation Society,
with thanks for all their assistance*

Random House ⌂ New York

Text copyright © 1997 by Joyce Milton. Illustrations copyright © 1997 by Bryn Barnard.
All rights reserved under International and Pan-American Copyright Conventions.
Published in the United States by Random House, Inc., New York, and simultaneously
in Canada by Random House of Canada Limited, Toronto.

Photo credits: Ronald H. Cohn/The Gorilla Foundation, 43; © Wildlife Conservation Society (Bronx Zoo), 47.

http://www.randomhouse.com/

Library of Congress Cataloging-in-Publication Data
Milton, Joyce. Gorillas: gentle giants of the forest/by Joyce Milton ; illustrated by Bryn Barnard.
p. cm. — (Step into reading. A Step 2 book)
ISBN 0-679-87284-1 (pbk.) — ISBN 0-679-97284-6 (lib. bdg.) 1. Gorillas—Juvenile literature.
[1. Gorillas.] I. Barnard, Bryn, ill. II. Title. III. Series: Step into reading. Step 2 book.
QL737.P96M56 1997 599.88—dc20 94-41839

Printed in the United States of America 10 9 8 7 6 5 4 3 2 1

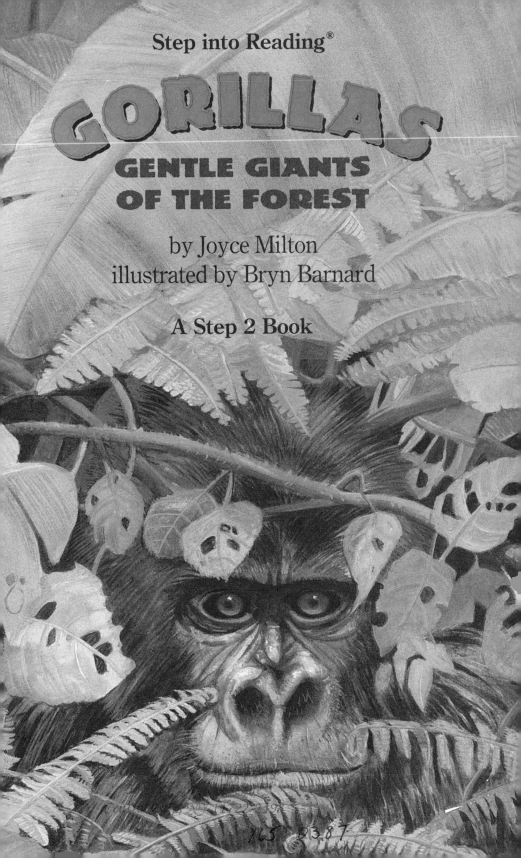

Step into Reading®

GORILLAS

GENTLE GIANTS
OF THE FOREST

by Joyce Milton
illustrated by Bryn Barnard

A Step 2 Book

765 2387

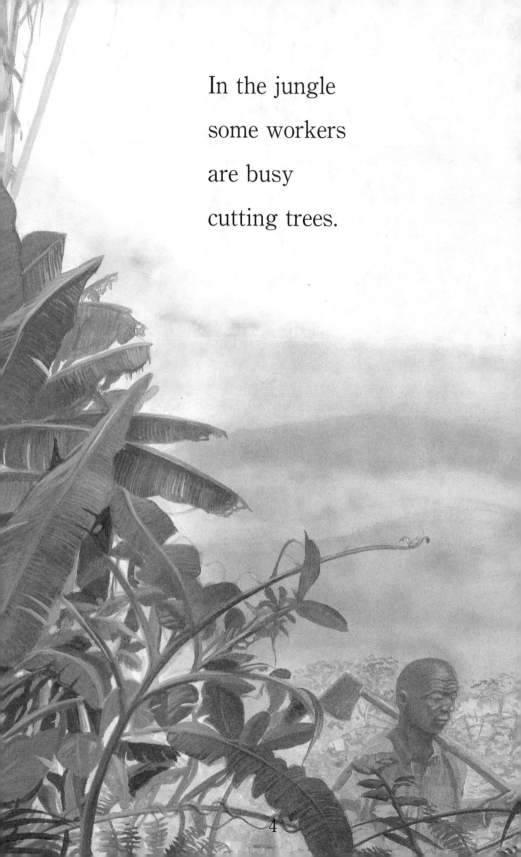

In the jungle
some workers
are busy
cutting trees.

4

They don't know it,
but up the hill
a family of gorillas
is taking
its noontime nap.

The biggest gorilla

opens one eye.

He hears the workers' shouts.

Suddenly he jumps up,

slaps his chest,

and lets out a loud scream—

RRRRRR-AAHHHEEE!

That scream is

one of the scariest sounds

in the world.

It says: KEEP AWAY—OR ELSE!

The workers drop their tools

and run for their lives!

A male gorilla
can weigh 500 pounds.
That's more than
twice as much
as a grown man.
The gorilla is also
many times stronger!

He can snap
a tree branch in half
with his teeth.
His arms are long
and powerful.
When he spreads them wide,
they stretch for eight feet.

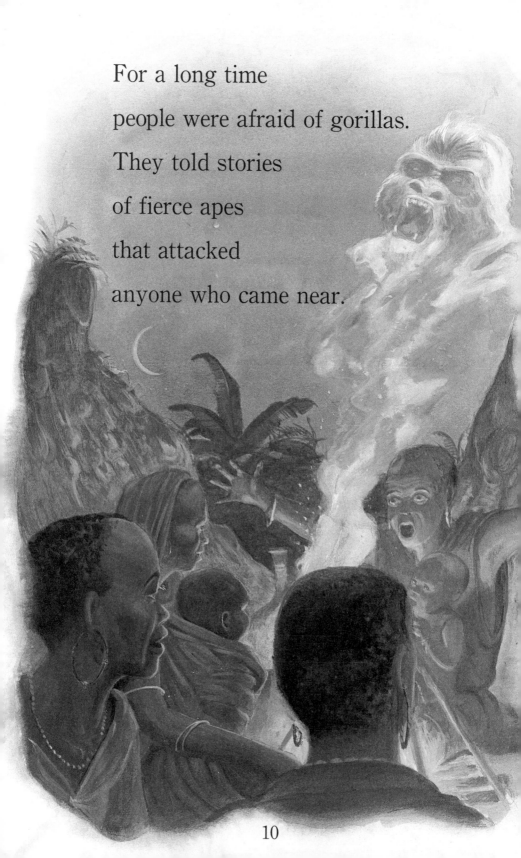

For a long time
people were afraid of gorillas.
They told stories
of fierce apes
that attacked
anyone who came near.

A few scientists
wondered if
the stories were true.
They decided
to go into the African forests
and see for themselves.

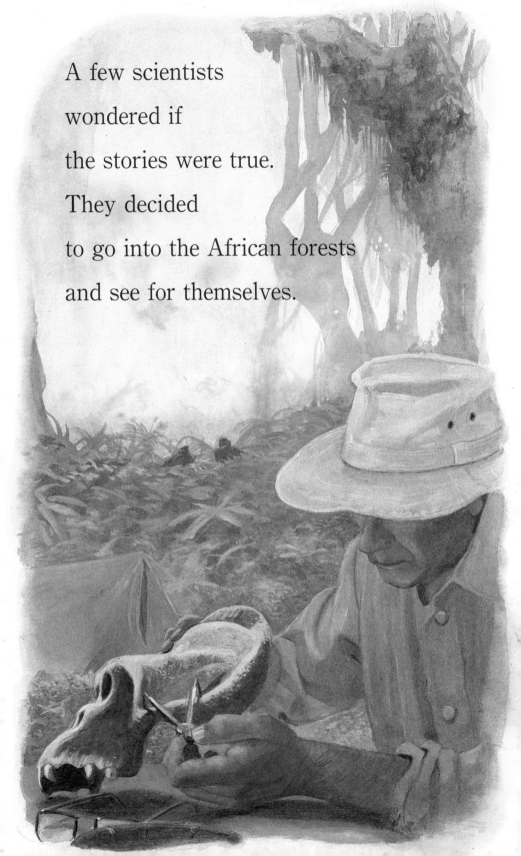

At first the scientists
were afraid.
But they learned
not to show it.
Why?

If you run from a gorilla,

he may chase you and bite you.

But his charge is mostly bluff.

If you meet a gorilla,

you have to stand still

and pretend

you aren't scared.

Then he will

stop charging

and run

right past you.

Dian Fossey
was one of the first
to study wild gorillas.
To make them trust her,
she tried to act
like a gorilla.
She scratched herself
and thumped her chest.
She grunted and chewed leaves.

Once, when a gorilla
charged her,
Dian made an ugly face.
The gorilla
was so surprised
he stopped in his tracks
and sat down.

After a while the gorillas
got used to Dian.
One young male—
Dian called him Peanuts—
was very curious.
He came closer and closer.
Dian stretched out her hand
and lay still.

Very gently
Peanuts touched her fingers.
Dian was so excited
she almost cried.
She was the first human
ever to be touched
by a wild gorilla!

By watching gorillas up close,
Dian and other scientists
found out what they
are really like.

Gorillas are
gentle creatures.
They live quietly
in groups.
The leader
is an older male.
Scientists call him
a silverback.
He gets his name
from the silvery gray hairs
on his back and neck.

Young male gorillas
are called blackbacks.
In the group
they are followers.

When a blackback
is nine or ten years old,
his hair
starts to turn gray.
In a few years
he will become
a silverback.
Then he may
stay with the group
or wander off on his own.

Female gorillas are
half as big as males.
They spend their time
taking care of their babies.
When a baby gorilla is born,
it weighs four or five pounds.
Its skin is smooth
and hairless.

When the group moves
from place to place,
the mother carries her baby
in one arm.

The baby drinks
her mother's milk
and grows strong.
When she is
two months old,
she is ready to ride
on her mother's back.

She holds tight
to the long hairs.
But sometimes
she loses her grip
and falls—OOPS!

This silverback
is leading his group
through the forest,
looking for breakfast.
The gorillas walk
single file
on all fours.
They rest their weight
on the backs of their fingers.
A gorilla can walk
on its hind legs, too.
But only for a few steps.

Soon the gorillas find
a patch of wild celery.
The celery is
fresh and sweet.

Breakfast takes
two or three hours.
Then it is time
for a nap.

In the afternoon
the gorillas will eat
another big meal.
They eat almost all day long.

Gorillas like many kinds
of wild plants.
Bamboo shoots. Ferns.
Tree bark. Wild blackberries.
Even scratchy nettles!

Around noon the group

settles down for a nap.

But one young gorilla

is wide awake

and ready to play.

He puts a leaf

on his head

just for fun.

Then a tiny frog
hops right under
his nose.
He chases after it.

In the trees nearby
a hungry leopard
is watching.
A young gorilla
would make a tasty meal.

Suddenly the silverback
wakes up.
He smells the leopard
and starts to hoot:
HOO—HOO—HOO!

He grabs a leaf

and holds it

between his lips.

When a gorilla does this,

watch out!

It means he is angry!

POK! POK! POK! POK!
The silverback
beats his chest.
Then he rips up
handfuls of grass
and throws them
into the air.
He runs sideways
on all fours.
What is he doing?
He is showing his stuff!
A silverback
will defend his group
to the death.

Even a leopard
won't fight
an angry silverback.
The big cat slinks away
into the forest.

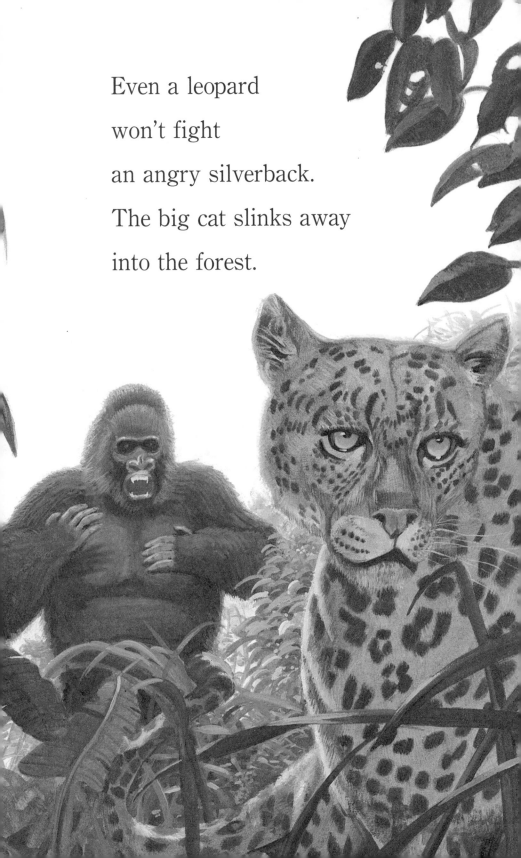

Just before sunset
the silverback
breaks up some bushes
and piles them
around him.
He is making a nest!

All gorillas sleep in nests.
Every night
the young gorillas
build new nests
in the branches of a tall tree.
The older gorillas
are too heavy
to climb trees.
They make their nests
on the ground.
The mothers cuddle
with their babies.

Are gorillas smart?
For a long time
most scientists
didn't think so.
Now a gorilla named Koko
is proving them wrong.
When Koko was a baby,
a scientist named
Penny Patterson
became her teacher.
Penny taught Koko
the same sign language
used by deaf people.
Koko has learned about 2,000 words.
She even makes up new words.
Koko calls broccoli *stink food*.
She calls a mask an *eye hat*.

Koko can do many things
a child can do.
She likes to look
at picture books.
She plays
with her pet dog, Flower.
She is even learning
to read.

But there is one thing
Koko can't do—
she can't talk.
So Penny gave her a computer
that talks for her.
By watching how Koko
uses her computer,
scientists will find out
how all gorillas
think and learn.

Koko at her computer.

No one knows the future
of the wild gorillas.
The African countries
where they live
are poor and crowded.
People need land
for farms and villages.

They are chopping down
the great forests
where the gorillas live.
Many Africans want
to save the gorillas.
But they need help.

Today more than 300 gorillas live in American zoos. They mate and have babies just like wild gorillas.

Omani was born

in a zoo in New York City.

Her mother was born in a zoo, too.

Will Omani's grandchildren

live in zoos?

Maybe not.

Maybe someday the

forests will be saved.

*Omani at
21 months.*

Then Omani's grandchildren might live free in the wild!